First World War
and Army of Occupation
War Diary
France, Belgium and Germany

15 DIVISION
Divisional Troops
225 Machine Gun Company
10 July 1917 - 28 February 1918

WO95/1930/3

The Naval & Military Press Ltd
www.nmarchive.com
Published in association with The National Archives

Published by

The Naval & Military Press Ltd

Unit 10 Ridgewood Industrial Park,

Uckfield, East Sussex,

TN22 5QE England

Tel: +44 (0) 1825 749494

www.naval-military-press.com

www.nmarchive.com

This diary has been reprinted in facsimile from the original. Any imperfections are inevitably reproduced and the quality may fall short of modern type and cartographic standards.

© **Crown Copyright**
Images reproduced by permission of The National Archives, London, England, 2015.

Contents

Document type	Place/Title	Date From	Date To
Heading	WO95/1930/3		
Heading	BEF 15 Div Troops 225 M.G. Coy 1917 July To 1918 Feb		
War Diary	Belton Park Grantham	10/07/1917	10/07/1917
War Diary	Grantham	11/07/1917	11/07/1917
War Diary	Southampton	11/07/1917	11/07/1917
War Diary	Havre	12/07/1917	18/07/1917
War Diary	Montrolier-Buchy	18/07/1917	18/07/1917
War Diary	Abbeville	18/07/1917	18/07/1917
War Diary	Poperinghe	19/07/1917	19/07/1917
War Diary	Brandhoek	19/07/1917	24/07/1917
War Diary	Ecole	24/07/1917	28/07/1917
War Diary	Brandhoek	29/07/1917	30/07/1917
War Diary	Millcots	31/07/1917	31/07/1917
Heading	War Diary of 225 Machine Gun Company From 1 August 1917 To 31 August 1917 Volume (2)		
War Diary	Millcots	01/08/1917	03/08/1917
War Diary	Brandhoek	04/08/1917	04/08/1917
War Diary	Winnizeele	05/08/1917	08/08/1917
War Diary	Toronto Camp	09/08/1917	09/08/1917
War Diary	Ramparts	10/08/1917	13/08/1917
War Diary	Vlamertinghe	14/08/1917	17/08/1917
War Diary	Ramparts	18/08/1917	21/08/1917
War Diary	Ecole	21/08/1917	31/08/1917
Heading	War Diary of 225 M.G. Company From 1 Sept To 30 Sept 1917 Volume 3		
War Diary	Watou	01/09/1917	01/09/1917
War Diary	Watou Arras	02/09/1917	02/09/1917
War Diary	Tilloy-Les-Hermaville	03/09/1917	06/09/1917
War Diary	St. Nicholas (Fife camp)	07/09/1917	17/09/1917
War Diary	Fife Camp	18/09/1917	30/09/1917
Miscellaneous	Appendix I Operation Orders No. 102 Ref Map as before	10/09/1917	10/09/1917
Heading	War Diary of 225 Company Machine Gun Corps From 1 October 1917 To 31 October 1917 Volume 4		
War Diary	Fife Camp	01/10/1917	13/10/1917
War Diary	Arras	14/10/1917	31/10/1917
Heading	War Diary of 225th Company, M.G. Corps. From 1 Nov 1917 To 30 Nov 1917 (Volume 5)		
War Diary	Arras	01/11/1917	30/11/1917
Heading	War Diary of 225th Coy M.G. Corps From 1st December 1917 To 31st December. 1917 (Volume 6)		
War Diary	Arras	01/12/1917	31/12/1917
Heading	War Diary of 225th M.G. Company From 1st January 1918 To 31st January 1918 (Volume 7)		
War Diary	Arras	01/01/1918	02/01/1918
War Diary	Dainville	03/01/1918	31/01/1918
Heading	War Diary of 225th Coy. M.G. Corps. From 1st Feb. 1918 To 28th Feb. 1918 (Volume 8)		
War Diary	Dainville	01/02/1918	05/02/1918

| War Diary | Arras | 06/02/1918 28/02/1918 |
| Miscellaneous | Operation-Ypres-31.7.17. To 4.8.17. Machine Guns. | |

W 895/1930/3

BEF

15 Div Troops

225 M.G. Coy.

1917 July to 1918 Feb

Army Form C. 2118

225 M G Coy

No 1

WAR DIARY
or
INTELLIGENCE SUMMARY.
(Erase heading not required.)

Instructions regarding War Diaries and Intelligence Summaries are contained in F. S. Regs., Part II. and the Staff Manual respectively. Title pages will be prepared in manuscript.

Place	Date	Hour	Summary of Events and Information	Remarks and references to Appendices
BELTON PARK GRANTHAM	10/7/17	10 P.M.	Left camp for railway station GRANTHAM	J.A. Cpt
GRANTHAM	11/7/17	12-30 AM	Entrained & left station	J.A. Cpt
SOUTHAMPTON	11/7/17	8-30 AM	Arrived at docks, 4 miles out for high winds.	J.A. "
"	11/7/17	4-30 PM	Embarked on S.S. AUSTRALIND.	J.A. "
"	11/7/17	6 PM	Sailed.	J.A. "
HAVRE	12/7/17	4-30 AM	Arrived.	J.A. "
"	12/7/17	6 PM	Arrived Rest Camp No 1.	J.A. "
"	13/7/17	9 AM	Arms, Box Helmets & Teeth Inspection	J.A. "
"	13/7/17	10 AM	M.O.'s Inspection	J.A. "
"	14/7/17	10 AM	64829 Pte WHITE to Hospital (Arms)	
"	14-17 7/17	Various	Gun Drill, Bretley Parades, Squad Drill Inspection, Also 4 mile Surplice Kits sent to SOUTHAMPTON	J.A. Cpt & returned
"	17/7/17	9 PM	Orders for entraining received	J.A. "
"	18/7/17	6:30 AM	Left No 1 Rest Camp	J.A. "
"	18/7/17	8 AM	Entrained at Point 3	J.A. "
"	18/7/17	10-17 AM	Train departed	J.A. "
MONTROLIER- BROMY	18/7/17	3 PM	Train arrived. Stopped 30 mins for men's tea travelling & feeding animals	J.A. "
"	18/7/17	8-30 PM	Train arrived. Stopped 30 mins for do	J.A. "
ABBEVILLE	19/7/17		Train arrived	J.A. "
POPERINGHE	19/7/17	5-45 PM	Arrived new camp.	J.A. "
BRANDHOEK	19/7/17	9 AM	Escort new camp at Q.12.B.25. O.C. Coy with 2/Lt GROVE & 1 Sergeant reached trenches with Devon.	J.A. "
			M.G. Office 2/Lt Peterkin with men from each section proceeded to trenches at 1-30 p.m. for 48 hrs tour of duty. They were instructed to fire runaway fire during the night to -200 to junction	J.A. "
			M. 10 first. Some gas shells were sent for this area.	

Army Form C. 2118.

WAR DIARY
or
INTELLIGENCE SUMMARY.
(Erase heading not required.)

Instructions regarding War Diaries and Intelligence Summaries are contained in F. S. Regs., Part II. and the Staff Manual respectively. Title pages will be prepared in manuscript.

Place	Date	Hour	Summary of Events and Information	Remarks and references to Appendices
BRANDHOEK	20/7/17	10 a.m.	Moved to new camp. 4 Officers & 4 N.C.O.s proceeded to trenches for instruction. Both parties encountered heavy shell fire, entering YPRES. Heavy gas shelling in front area during the night.	J.F. Cpl.
"	22/7/17	7.30 pm.	Weather fine. Party to guns at rifle inspection during the day. Returns 2 & 3 (S.6 M.R.) with their guns etc. and their Section returned after relieve No. 44 Coy in trenches. Hand Quarters ECOLE outside YPRES. 2 other Sections in WEST LANE T & H. ST JAMES TRENCH. Party & & M.G. transport returned safely.	J.F. Cpl. J.F. Cpl
"	23/7/17	4 a.m.	Enemy aeroplane flew over camps firing machine guns at them & dropping bombs. They succeeded in hitting No. stores. DRIVER CLARKE F. 30266 admitted to hospital suffering from abrasions.	J.F. Cpl.

Army Form C. 2118.

WAR DIARY
or
INTELLIGENCE SUMMARY.
(Erase heading not required.)

Place	Date	Hour	Summary of Events and Information	Remarks and references to Appendices
BRANDHOEK	23/7/17	4 a.m	E.A bombed Camps in vicinity & also dropped bombs. Quiet all day in camp. Machine Guns in trenches carried out during the night harassing fire on enemy's lines of communication, gaps in wire etc.	J.I.
"	24/7/17	7 p.m	No: 1 & 4 sections left camp to relieve No: 2 & 3 in the trenches. Relief completed by 3 a.m 25/7/17	J.I.
		8	O.C. Coy. took up residence in ECOLE, leaving reported to O.C 146 Brigade at 7 P.M1P4075 YPRES on the way up.	
ECOLE	"	1-45p.m	27308 Pte. BURKE. J.L. Shrapnel wound in left shoulder about 1-45 p.m. during a hot barrage put up by our infantry in aid of a successful raid carried out on enemy trenches.	J.I.
	"	5-45pm.	29646 Pte. JOHNSON. L.W. shrapnel wound, left arm.	
ECOLE	25/7/17	4-5-30 a.m.	Heavy shelling with H.E & Phos shells, including the new mustard oil shell, deployed No: 2 & 3 sections during ECOLE after being relieved from trenches.	J.I.
			85799 Pte THOMPSON. S. Gassed on way back to camp.	
			82204 Pte WILSON. O. Phosgene shrapnel wound, left leg.	
	10-1pm.		Heavy shelling of HALF MOON TRENCH & vicinity with numerous casualties to troops in Keep.	J.I.
	2-2-12 pm.		Our 4" guns in SOOTH LANE sent down a trench barrage in conjunction with artillery according to schedule.	
	10 pm.		Harassing fire continued each night according to programme.	
			Heavy gas shelling around ST JAMES TRENCH	
ECOLE	26/7/17	a.m	Gas shells in ST JAMES TRENCH followed by heavy shells at shelters. Three of our his Ration party encountered severe shelling with H.E & Gas shells & water cart & stretcher had to be left here on account of heavy fire. A shell burst by 9th GROVE who just escaped being hit into to explosion of several shells in our camp. Treated by R.O.W.C. for shell shock forwarded to Field Hospital. Started in Ambulance bus on his way down & fell out & reported to Coy Commander. Returned to Unit (Brandhoek) suffering from deafness & shock.	J.I.

Army Form C. 2118.

WAR DIARY
or
INTELLIGENCE SUMMARY.
(Erase heading not required.)

Instructions regarding War Diaries and Intelligence Summaries are contained in F. S. Regs., Part II, and the Staff Manual respectively. Title pages will be prepared in manuscript.

Place	Date	Hour	Summary of Events and Information	Remarks and references to Appendices
ECOLE	27.7.17	2 a.m.	2 & 3 Sections relieved 1 & 4 in the trenches. No 3 Section sustained following casualties during relief. 82946 Pte Crow W killed. 22936 Pte Horsfall C, 102251 Hpl Powell J, 45947 Pte Payne, wounded. 1 & 4 Sections returned to Camp.	OR
		3.15 p.m.	Enemy shelled SCHOOL with H.E. 89043 Pte Mahon wounded R Leg	
		10 p.m.–12 m.n.	Gun positions heavily shelled. Gunners escaped without casualty.	
ECOLE	28.7.17	5 a.m.	Practice barrage fired down at 5 a.m. during which No 95392 Pte READ F was killed. 85072 Pte MITCHELL J wounded. 27080 L/Cpl ENGLAND C grazed but remained with unit.	
		7 p.m.	Raid by 2 Coys. Raid successful. About 50 prisoners. During barrage No 32 P4 Pte SWINDLE T wounded R hand slight. No retaliation from enemy	
		11 a.m.	ECOLE heavily shelled	
BRANDHOEK	29.7.17	5 a.m.	Camp bombed by E.A. no damage to Coy.	
		6 p.m.	O.C. Coy returned from Trenches. No 108869 Pte Curtis G present (wounded, did)	OR
do	30.7.17	1 & 4 Sections returned to Trenches No 1 annexed POTIJZE DEFENCES via C TRACK	
		at 11.30 p.m. instructed men to gun pits in wall Lotus behind the STRONG POINT.	
		No 4 Section manned up in margin from to Tr 28.6" B.d. & took up a position in the POTIJZE DEFENCES. No 2 Section in SOUTH LANE No 3 SECTION in SOUTH + WEST LANE	
MILLCOT	31.7.17		No 1 Section in POTIJZE STRONG POINT. At evening "Stand to Section before went forward & connected up Barrage Position	
		No 2 Section in SOUTH LANE 1/4 gun from No 2 Section forward up the Infantry. 2 gun under 2/Lt DAVIS + two under 2/Lt RIRK. The former took up a position on the Black Line just in front of WILDE WOOD. 2/Lt RIRK took 2 guns to the Black Line & took up a position	

8 AUG 1917

WAR DIARY
or
INTELLIGENCE SUMMARY.

Place	Date	Hour	Summary of Events and Information	Remarks and references to Appendices
MILL COT	31/7/17		About 200 yds in front of FREZENBERG REDOUBT at H.25.d.0.7. the BLACK WATCH holding the line and the 45" Inf Bde being relieved on the front line about 4084h. in front formed nothing seeing & being compelled to the 45" Bde retired on the Black Line which very prominent met the firm but No 3 section remained in reserve in Limit Line. No 4 Section took up a position up to as soon from C to the HQ'A.K. in H.20.7.1.25 Defences. Three rifleman then heavily shelled	

8 AUG 1917

CONFIDENTIAL

War Diary

of

225 Machine Gun Company

from 1 August 1917 to 31 August 1917

Volume (2)

WAR DIARY or INTELLIGENCE SUMMARY

Army Form C. 2118.

Place	Date	Hour	Summary of Events and Information	Remarks and references to Appendices
MILL COTS	11/9/17		No 1 Section ordered forward to BLUE LINE. Heavy enemy shelling on way up to B.C. Enemy wounded — from period in rear of aid tour behind a hedge between GREY RUIN and POTIJZE ROAD. Spent sometime assist to BAVARIA HOUSE. Stretcher bearers in front of BLUE LINE Huns [?] and arrangements made with Off. SCOTTISH RIFLES to send guns forward to be touch of attack. Our position heavily shelled. No 2 Section reported enemy trench attack. Being driven off by M.G. & LEWIS gun fire. By 6 am situation quiet with exception of M.G.s & Snipers hidden out informs. Casualties — 4/2c B.B. Davis killed. No 3 Section in reserve in SOUTH LANE cleaning guns &c. No 4 Section ordered C moved 10th up to Junction near GREY RUINS in order to be able to put indirect fire on enemy trenches. O.C. Infantry ordered Section to take up positions in to GREY RUINS STRONG POINT to proceed to place direct fire on the enemy should any get through during a counter attack. Section severely shelled. Casualties — 2/Lt GROVE badly wounded Sgt ALDRED killed Pte STAGG and other 2 guns put out of action.	
do	12/9/17		No 1 Section reported heavy enemy shelling all day. S.O.S. sent up on left group put out action. Enemy dropped barrage from battleaxe until seven stretchers attd by teams from forward for their fire. Enemy heavier than Off Sutton shelling no casualties. No 2 Section reported still enemy trench very bad Lieut wounded by M.G. fire & Sandford	

Army Form C. 2118.

WAR DIARY
or
INTELLIGENCE SUMMARY.
(Erase heading not required.)

Instructions regarding War Diaries and Intelligence Summaries are contained in F. S. Regs., Part II. and the Staff Manual respectively. Title pages will be prepared in manuscript.

Place	Date	Hour	Summary of Events and Information	Remarks and references to Appendices
MILL COT	2/8/17		No 3 Section received orders from B.M. E and 2 guns to report to 7" CAMERONS 2 guns had received orders already. Men sent to 7th CAMERONS by Capt BARRETT 4th (K.M.G. Coy) Returned 2/Lt JENKINS 44th M.G. Coy in front of WILDEWOOD Shelling very intense intense men with the 6th guns in shelter afters numbers un	
			BILL COT No 4 Section in GREN RUIN STRONG POINT	
do	3/8/17		No 1 Section reported without losses shelling during day Emplacements were there 2/Lt ALEXANDER wounded Pte ROBINSON + ALLAN wounded tent remaining with unit	
		10pm	Returned to Camp at BRANDHOEK No 2 Section reported their 6 post during movement were seen on the enemy line about 1400x away + shelled C was called two + Counsel over to be attacks before taking away wounded. Rained all day	
		7pm	2 guns of No 2 Section relieved by 4/5" M.G. Coy Section proceeded to camp w BRANDHOER. No 3 Section still at WILDEWOOD 2/C PALMER sick went with two first McSAWYER	
		4pm	wounded by shell Section relieved from camps + to LINDI NODE + gun in A44" M.G. Coy Headrs. Section returned to camp (BRANDHOEK) No 4 Section returned to Camp (BRANDHOEK)	

8 Army Form C. 2118.

WAR DIARY
or
INTELLIGENCE SUMMARY.
(Erase heading not required.)

Place	Date	Hour	Summary of Events and Information	Remarks and references to Appendices
BRANDHOEK	4/9/17	4 pm	Company entrained for WINNIZEELE. 2/m.C went on in advance to arrange billets. Took for arms that new bivouac until 11 AM	
WINNIZEELE	5/9/17		Company settling down cleaning up & refitting	
do	6/9/17		Company inspection. Lewis gun equipment & instruction of Lieut T.G.m Highwood & Wearing of uniforms. New Lewis teams instructed & oiled.	
do	7/9/17		Gas respirators P.H. Helmets etc. Inspection. 2/Lt Gill joined the Coy for duty.	
do	8/9/17	10 am	Entrained for Toronto Camp. Arrived there 12.180. Took over duties from new battn to 16th Division	
TORONTO CAMP	9/9/17	7 pm	Company moved off in motor lorries for Asylum YPRES where guides were waiting for them (Coy H.Q RAMPARTS 2nd in C WINZIG COTS 2/Lt FINNIGAN joined the Coy. No 1 Section at SQUARE FARM, No 4 FREZENBURG CROSSROADS, No 2	
RAMPARTS	10/9/17		200 yds behind FREZENBERG REDOUBT, No 3 at BILL COT, Relief completed without casualties. 2 teams of No 2 Section were unable to relieve until following night owing to out point being just by hard luck.	
RAMPARTS	11/9/17		Section ration party being shelled by enemy during the night. Enemy with westerly wind & our teams were engaged in company of S.O.S. from BANARINHOUSE to farmhouse. Our guns then on S.O.S firing at & carrying out harassing fire on tracks. No 4 section following casualties. 6720 Pte WILKINSON 99355 Pte MICKLEJOHN. 57125 Pte PRINCE all wounded. No 1 Sec reports one gun and tripod blown up.	

A5834 Wt.W4973/M687 750,000 8/16 D.D. & L. Ltd. Forms/C.2118/13

Army Form C. 2118.

WAR DIARY
or
INTELLIGENCE SUMMARY.
(Erase heading not required.)

Instructions regarding War Diaries and Intelligence Summaries are contained in F.S. Regs., Part II. and the Staff Manual respectively. Title pages will be prepared in manuscript.

Place	Date	Hour	Summary of Events and Information	Remarks and references to Appendices
RAMPARTS	12/9/17	4.25am	Lieut. No.1 reports that troops (ours) were opened on S.O.S signal going up, but word received from HQ in front that there were no enemy attack. Learnt fire work from our emplacements improved - men on sentries. No.2 listen report heavy shelling by enemy on left front known of enemy unfriendly actions.	
		4.20am	No.3 listen report that S.O.S signal going up game shower from their shelling by enemy. Dug out partially blown in but no casualties owing to later. The following casualties observed in the trenches - Sgt Vogts bad wound of murderer (sent to Hospital) Pt WHALL ammunition (sent to Hospital). No.2 Lr 2/4 MATTHEWS wounded No.3 Lt 87325 Pt OVERLAND 103496 Pt PEDDAR both wounded accidentally Pt PEDDAR slightly & remaining with unit No.4 Lr 2/4 HOWELLS wounded & arms & shoulder 9023 Pt PRITCHETT wounded (since died)	MA
RAMPARTS	13/9/17	4am	2/E BILL arrived from transport lines. Turn up here to tile dumps & No 4 station No.1 Le. where S.O signal went up. Some quiet but swoody respinsl from Hy in front. No attack. Cursed first from Sid (and about 1/4 kilo east SQUARE FARM reported to to twice attack by enemy. 2 emplacements slightly damaged 1 Lewis gun sent to No.1 Lietein (lent by HQ N & Coy) to replace damaged one 9/11 PRITCHARD proceed (from transport lines) to Hospital	M

WAR DIARY
or
INTELLIGENCE SUMMARY.

(Erase heading not required.)

Army Form C. 2118.

Instructions regarding War Diaries and Intelligence Summaries are contained in F. S. Regs., Part II. and the Staff Manual respectively. Title pages will be prepared in manuscript.

Place	Date	Hour	Summary of Events and Information	Remarks and references to Appendices
RAMPARTS	15/9/17		No 2 Station report heavy shelling by enemy. Enemy aircraft very active during the evening flying low. Rumours regarding (?) advance 2 kts. No. 3 Station reports heavy shelling by own & enemy artillery. No S.O.S. signal or other relief in daylight. Enemy being shelled. No. 4 Station report retaliation fairly quiet. All Stations have been sending S.O.S. up to this hour on return when daylight	
VLAMERTINGHE	16/9/17	3pm	Transport lines moved to HEAD Hrs & Lorks taken over	
		12 mn	Boy miscued spanned train to camp. All Station ready to Camp as 8am as P.D. out everything if taking of No.2 Section. No casualties during day.	
VLAMERTINGHE	16/9/17		Company resting. Relieving ch. Camp shelled by hourly at intervals	
– do –		6am	Boy shelling up into of difference being made during Camp during intervals	
		5 H.V guns during the night. No casualties - also shelling by day. Remained 2 guns during forenoon & afternoon	
– do –	17/9/17		Boy warned for line Section Y.S.T. at sunset 16 & 7pm U.C. Coy & 2nd line	
		11pm	at RAMPARTS – 9/20 PETERKIN KIRK & ASHBURNER remaining in Camp. Relief complete by 400 8th Section in IBEX RESERVE and BULL COTTAGE	
RAMPARTS	18/9/17	2am	Relief completed by No 1 Section (8/20 F INNIGAN) to FROEZENBURG REDOUBT No 1 Station report that under instructions from 2/4 M.G. Coy that only four gun when S.O.S. signal sent up. Very heavy shelling by enemy No. 2 Section report not being able to by enemy Pte POLLARD No 105900 wounded in neck	

A 5834 Wt. W4973/M687 750,000 8/16 D. D. & L. Ltd. Forms/C.2118/13

WAR DIARY
or
INTELLIGENCE SUMMARY
(Erase heading not required.)

Army Form C. 2118.

Place	Date	Hour	Summary of Events and Information	Remarks and references to Appendices
RAMPARTS	19/9/17	4.45 am	No 1 Pigeon Post having been suddenly silenced. Enemy aircraft was particularly active	
		5.30 am	Sniper active. Enemy M. gun firing from approx a position 30° during E of N from probably POMMERN CASTLE active at dusk & dawn	
		6-12 am	No 3 Section report shelling by enemy. Immediately round FREZENBERG and STATION BUILDINGS. also the Railway Ground to West from the right. SB	
		1.45 am	enemy appeared to fire a DUMP in direction of MILLCOT	
		(-9.30 pm)	enemy aircraft very active	
		4.46 am	S.O.S signal went up which could seen on left though to be gas being pumped in direction of the enemy	
	20.9.17	4.45 am	No 4 Section report No 13 gun fired 300 rounds, ammunition not then broke putting gun out of action	
			(Cpl) SIBBONS & Dr. PRATT reported from Hospital.	
			Enemy put a lot of gas shells between IBEX RESERVE and WILDE WOOD and shelled on Railway	
		8 am	2 enemy pigeons flew very low coming from open ground in front of low flying in Funn	
			2 of our pigeons brought down in enemy lines. No 2 Station arrived from Cast ? gone in as Ws.	
do	21.9.17	9 pm	Coy H Q moved to ECOLE following proceedings:	

No. 10877 Pte DICK + Pte 926 Pte ROWE
2/x PETERKIN arrived from Cast? Team in charge of gun taken over in the line

No 10877/ Pte DICK + Pte 926 Pte ROWE to Pass

A5834 Wt. W4973/M687 750,000 8/16 D. D. & L. Ltd. Forms/C.2118/13

WAR DIARY or INTELLIGENCE SUMMARY

Army Form C. 2118.

Place	Date	Hour	Summary of Events and Information	Remarks and references to Appendices
ECOLE	21.9.17		Coy turned out 2 Lieut*s* A Battery to I.6.c.45.15. B Battery to I.12.90.15. B Battery afterwards moved to a position N of BILL COT. Enemy artillery was active during the night, firing 20 minutes bursts of about 1 bd per 4 minutes - about 250 bells fired. A Battery area was shelled. B Battery was shelled with 5.9". Casualties nil. Work and preparations during half moon fatigues june shiftied on S.O.S. line M.24.B.91. LT SIMPSON and guard down to Camp (R BROOKES). Carrying party of 2 N.C.O's & 25 O.R. attached from Infantry to Coy. S.A.A training up to Battery.	(A)
ditto	22.9.17		B Battery has been fairly heavily shelled & has slightly increased their dispersion with bits out of two B Forest. A wounded Lieut subsequently killed was brought down. Orders received from Division that "B" Battery was relieved to reinforce "B" Bd and A Battery on defensive of 46" Bde gun positions and changed their areas which cover new front. Several gun teams used during the night by A Battery in trench. Guns fired about 4 bells per gun at a rate of 2 bds per hour. Fairly heavy shelling by enemy. Ammunition now in gun positions 100 GS rounds in addition to 16 bells per gun filled. Following men wounded to Camp sick No RH976 Pte W.N.E (infantry) No 18572 W.A POTTS (infantry) No 57356 L/Sgt Green (infantry)	(B)

WAR DIARY or INTELLIGENCE SUMMARY

Army Form C. 2118.

Place	Date	Hour	Summary of Events and Information	Remarks and references to Appendices
ECOLE	23.9.17		2/Lt SPRAGG joined at transport lines	
-do-	24.9.17		Sgt WEEDON sick to hospital from transport lines. Boy now at disposal of 45th Bde carrying out harassing fire on tracks used by enemy ration party. S.A.A. & gun munition 190,000 rounds	
-do-	25.9.17		1 Offr (2/Lt COLE) and 17 O.R. joined at transport lines. Total S.A.A. expended 20,000 rounds. Enemy put up proofs of very lights in our direction when our M.G. fire opened. Retaliation by enemy artillery without causing damage. No. 64824 2/Lt BARR sick and to Hospital.	
		11pm	Guns were opened for on enemy motors and artillery and found at barrage speed for about 30 minutes then concentrated on harassing fire on remainder of night. Enemy assembly for from but no damage. 2PD29 Lt ROBINSON W.H. slightly wounded in thigh.	
-do-	26.9.17		No. 3 Section moved up to DOUGLAS VILLA. Total S.A.A. 67 pm munition 157,000 rounds. Artillery fire seemed somewhat intensified on FREZENBERG RIDGE then off Railway Junction. Two enemy trains were up during the day; two came down. About 11pm harassing fire was kept up during the night. 110,000 rounds being fired. Heavy rain fell and condition as gun position was bad	

WAR DIARY or INTELLIGENCE SUMMARY

Army Form C. 2118.

Place	Date	Hour	Summary of Events and Information	Remarks and references to Appendices
ECOLE	27/8/17		Officer i/c T.M.O.R reported from Transport lines	
		2/am	Our guns were opened with artillery in putting down barrage in to standard running out of 3 belts per gun were maintained whist 2 guns firing intermittently to between us until two strength intact on our right flank. The barrage from about 5 to 5.05 (zero to 5 past) changed to slow firing from the night to IDEN RESERVE. Harassing fire were kept up thro' the night. 12.30 enemy bombing attack from our right flank thrown back. Traces of enemy aeroplanes and infant were recorded and Casualties: No.BASON 2/Lt HUDSON wounded by shell (wound leg legs). 10226 Sjt PERKINS and 41STEVENS QMSy S. a.m. both (2) wounded, but both conditions good.	
ECOLE	28/8/17		Situation unchanged. Little no war aerial activity owing to stormy wind. During night 20,000 nds. fired as harassing fire. Made arrangements for relief which was expected during evening + all teams relieved to Bat. Reserve in ECOLE. Relieved in trenches by 4 S.W.B. M.G. Coy.	L.J.
ECOLE	29/8/17		Officers of relieving Battn (4.S.W.) came up to reconnoitre + learn all forward dispositions made for final relief of the place.	L.J.
ECOLE	30/8/17		Four dismounted returned to DADOS. Began to leave ECOLE in echelons at 3.30 pm for entraining at new NEAMERTINGE station. Got away from there by train before 6 pm and arrived at MATOY about 7.30 pm. Billeted in TRAPPIST FARM.	L.J.

Vol 3

CONFIDENTIAL

WAR DIARY

OF

225 M.G. COMPANY

FROM 1 Sep. to 30 Sep 1917

VOLUME 3

WAR DIARY
or
INTELLIGENCE SUMMARY.

Army Form C. 2118.

/5

Place	Date	Hour	Summary of Events and Information	Remarks and references to Appendices
WATOU	31/8/17		Spent quietly cleaning up and packing	
WATOU- ARRAS	2/9/17	3:30 a.m. Reveille. 3 a.m. 6 a.m. 5:30p/m 11 p.m.	Transport left for BAYINGCHOVE STATION at 4-30 a.m. Coy marched off from same place at 6 a.m. arrived station 10 a.m. and left for ARRAS at 11-31 a.m. Reaching here about 5-30 p.m. Marched to TILLOY-les-HERMAVILLE and arrived there about 11 p.m. where men got very comfortable billets. PTE SCOTT left us at WATOU very sick	
TILLOY-LES- HERMAVILLE	3/9/17		Spent morning Ceremony of Reveremento parade (2 Signallers met 6 Runners etc.) Cleaning equipment. Inspection of Lewises by Lieut. Commanders. Inspection of Rifles + anti air.	
—do—	4/9/17		Coy inspected by O.C. Coy. Major Hewitt. M.C. S.M.Y.O arrived	
—do—	5/9/17		Coy inspected by Brig. D.E. Coy. Lieuts making Inspections for same.	
—do—	6/9/17		8th Coy	
ST. NICHOLAS (FIFE CAMP)	7/9/17	7.15 am 2 pm	Coy marched to FIFE CAMP, ST. NICHOLAS. Camp taken over from 234 M.G. Coy. 1 + 2 Sections proceeded to trenches to relieve same of 232 Coy. N° 1 Section occupying P.14. (ref. map FAMPOUX 1/10000) P.12, P.13, P.15, + P.16. N° 2 Section P.17, P.18, R.10 + anti aircraft gun in CAMP TRENCH. Remainder of Coy in Reserve at FIFE CAMP. Capt FORESTER admitted (sick) to 17" Corps Officers Rest Camp. WARLUS.	
—do—	8/9/17		Parade in Camp 9.30 – 12.30 Drill etc. Section in line carried out humming fire	
—do—	9/9/17		Parade in Camp 9.30 – 12.30. Sections in line carried out usual humming fire 15" Gun Reuter Orders 1056 dated 9/9/17 N° 57296 Pte KELLY T + N° 99373 Pte KENNY J awarded the military medal	

Army Form C. 2118.

16

WAR DIARY
or
INTELLIGENCE SUMMARY.
(Erase heading not required.)

Instructions regarding War Diaries and Intelligence Summaries are contained in F. S. Regs., Part II. and the Staff Manual respectively. Title pages will be prepared in manuscript.

Place	Date	Hour	Summary of Events and Information	Remarks and references to Appendices
ST NICHOLAS FIFE CAMP	10/9/17		Parade in Camp 9.30 – 12.30. Lecture on Wire carried out. Harassing fire No P3387 Pt. Parade W. wounded (multiple gun shot wounds)	
~ do ~	11/9/17	9.30	Musical parade in Camp	
		9.30pm	Nos 1 & 2 Sections moved into new Battery positions Operation Order No 182 attached APPENDIX I	
~ do ~	12/9/17		Wired parades in Camp. Sections in new dugouts constructing shelter. Gun element sent down from gun line by night on L.O.S. signal only	
~ do ~	13/9/17		Wired parades in Camp. Sections in new constructing shelters during the day. Re. inforcement of 1 N.C.O. & 3 men arrived at Camp	
~ do ~	14/9/17	4pm	Nos 3 & 4 Sections relieved Nos 1 & 2 Sections in the Trenches	
~ do ~	15/9/17		Sections in the new front line completed with equipment shelters of a chemical nature. Wiring Parties were inspected by 2nd in C. Guns cleaned &c.	
~ do ~	16/9/17		Wired parades in Camp. Guns in line front arranging to synchronise. Guns cleaned &c.	
~ do ~	17/9/17	2.30pm	2/Lt L.E. GILL let on attachment to CORFO Trench Mortar Bid numbers Life on harassing station. Sections in line engaged by day in improving emplacements making dubouts. Harassing fire carried out. Visual harassing from camp at night. 2/Lt PETERKIN & Gr. RUSSELL proceeded to HAUTE AVENES for Infantry Course.	

WAR DIARY
or
INTELLIGENCE SUMMARY.
(Erase heading not required.)

Army Form C. 2118.

17

Place	Date	Hour	Summary of Events and Information	Remarks and references to Appendices
FIFE CAMP	18.9.17		Battalion in line working on wiring etc daily. Little to interrupt employment. Much interest in camp little aircraft activity.	
–do–	19.9.17	1.15pm & 7.35pm	Went continued on. Shells day into air.	
		4.30pm	Enemy fire shown a tendency about HARNESS'S RIFLE SUPPORT trenches. Retaliation about B in rear of S.O.S. firing up.	
		8 pm & 8.30 pm	Enemy renewed barrage on our line S.T.E. & MT. PLEASANT WOOD RIFLE SUPPORT, RLY EMBANKMENT & behind FAMPOUX. Aircraft activity on both sides. Several junction in camp. 1 O.R. joined from Base Depot.	
–do–	20.9.17	5 am	No. 8 station cannot but temporary about 500 rounds fired. No 1 station also cannot and barrage fire 1600 rounds fired. Strong area in SUNKEN ROAD informed from eng in degree. From stringth evened. Alternative locations for No 1 Battery above. 2 O.R. joined from Base Depot. 4 O.R.E. Hospital sick.	
–do–	21.9.17		1 + 2 stations relieved B + 2 in G. Emoder. Special function in HAPPY VALLEY selected from which to co-operate in raid on enemy by XII Division. Emplacements dug thereat. Angle + firm etc taken up at ouce. 4 O.R. joined from Base depot.	
–do–	22.9.17	4am	Eight from B 1 + 2 stations co-operated in 12" Hur. Raid by firing on SACK WOOD + DEVIL TRENCH.	
		2.30pm	39/A Bde being front. Casualties were evidently by enemy own civuialties NIL. 3 N.C.O. joined from Base Depot.	

Army Form C. 2118.

WAR DIARY
or
INTELLIGENCE SUMMARY.

(Erase heading not required.)

Instructions regarding War Diaries and Intelligence Summaries are contained in F.S. Regs., Part II. and the Staff Manual respectively. Title pages will be prepared in manuscript.

Place	Date	Hour	Summary of Events and Information	Remarks and references to Appendices
FIFE CAMP	23.9.17		Harassing fire carried out by Sections in the Trenches. Very lights were thrown up by the enemy. Work continued on dug outs.	EYR
~do~	24.9.17	4.30am	Enemy opened a heavy bombardment of our left front line. Sections stood to in readiness for S.O.S. signal. Bombardment lasted 25 minutes. Teams numerous for attack movement by the enemy. Situation in camp. Commenced work on ninth gun station in ARRAS.	EYR
~do~	25.9.17		Cpl ASHBY proceeded to AGNES LES DUISANS for gun course. Situation in camp normal but harassing shoots during the night. Enemy quiet on left front of division.	EYR
~do~	26.9.17		The enemy over a fairly heavy T.M bombardment on right of our own active area (this being been our position) at new station at 11.45 am. Situation in camp reported.	EYR
~do~	27.9.17		Harassing shoots carried out. Work continued on gun sites in the front line to new station. 3 O R to Hospital sick	EYR
~do~	28.9.17		Harassing shoots carried out. Enemy retaliated with M.G. & Shrapnel. War sentiment at new station. Capt FORESTER rejoined from Hospital	EYR
~do~	29.9.17		3 Other Ranks attended I.B.2 in the line. 2/Lt H.G. DYKE reported from Base. Situation quiet in line. Enemy brought line active. 2/Lt R.I.R.H - Lt MACDILL left for CAMIERS (M.G. Course)	EYR
~do~	30.9.17	10am	Enemy bombarded M/L PLOUVAIN. Batteries did not fire but let off red Rockets in each of enemy/company. Harassing fire carried out by the Programme. Recruits from 2/5 Div to work in communication trenches etc	EYR

A5834 Wt. W4973/M687 750,000 8/16 D.D. & L.Ltd. Forms/C.2118/13

SECRET.

APPENDIX I

Operation Orders No. 102
Ref Map as before

(1) No 1 Section 225 M.G. Coy will on the night of 11/12/15 quit the positions occupied by it at present & will move to positions that are being prepared for it at H 24 c 58. The men & officers must find room in the shafts in CHINSTRAP LANE. Orders for Sentries, etc; will be issued separately.

(2) No 2 Section will quit on night 11/12/15 the present positions & occupy positions that will be prepared for it in I 19 a 28.

(3) Section Officers will personally reconnoitre the route & the move will start at 9 p.m. 11/9 from old positions.

(4) Sub-Section Officers will be at H 24 c 58 & I 19 a 28 at 9 p.m. to meet officers from Nos. 3 & 4 Sections who will be preparing the emplacements.

(5) 2/Lt Field & 12 men of No. 3 will be prepared to start for work after 5 p.m. 2/Lt Finigan & 12 men of No. 4 will also be prepared.

(6) Arrangements for Trains will be issued later. 1 N.C.O. & 1 man will report to 2/Lt Field at 9 a.m. tomorrow.

(7) 2/Lt Gill report to Provost Bn Gordon Highlanders at 8.45 a.m. tomorrow with

measurements for T shaped bases. He will superintend construction of 8 of these & arrange for their delivery in camp by 5 p.m.

(8) Acknowledge.

Copies to O.C. No 1
 "   " " No 2
 "   " office

10/9/17.

Vol 4

CONFIDENTIAL

WAR DIARY

of

225 Company, Machine Gun Corps

From 1 October 1917   To 31 October 1917

Volume 4

Army Form C. 2118.

WAR DIARY
or
INTELLIGENCE SUMMARY.
(Erase heading not required.)

19

Place	Date	Hour	Summary of Events and Information	Remarks and references to Appendices
FIFE LANE & GRENADE	1/10/17		Work down to relieve our territory position. Enemy showing rifle on GRENADE & PEARL trenches also from present sentry outposts. Enemy flares fired. Casualties normal. Wind very light N. winds. Morning + afternoon. Wind carried our new trench.	C.V.A.
— do —	2/10/17		Camouflage work continued. Also dug out in SONKEN ROAD. Enemy rifle fire programme rounds refunded 2500. Situation normal. Casualties nil. Work continued at new trench. The following promoted to M.G. Belew CAMIERS 2/Lt. KIRK 59266 Sgt. McDill 17/88. Pte ROWDEN	C.V.A.
— " —	3/10/17		Work continued on new dug outs to shelter firing as per programme rounds expended 2250. Situation normal. Casualties nil. Wind light W & SW. Supply of S.A.A. normal.	C.V.A.
— " —	4/10/17		R.E. stores taken up from dump at ATHIES. Work for new trench continued. Work continued on dug outs. Also GUN TRENCH. Enemy shelling the right round expended 3000. A heavy bombardment by our artillery from 7pm to 10pm situation normal. Casualties nil. Wind strong W.	C.V.A.
— " —	5/10/17		1 + 2 batteries relieved 3 + 4 batteries in the line. New tramway lines for use. Target engaged as per programme rounds fired 1500. Situation normal. Casualties nil. 2/Lt H.S. COLE returned from hospital.	C.V.A.
— " —	6/10/17		Firing as per programme rounds expended 3250. Situation normal. Casualties nil. Weather dull & rainy. Report to War Diaries continued. 2/Lt H.F. COLE + B.Q.O.R. with transport proceeded to E.E.F. via MARSEILLES. G.O.R. arrived from Base School.	C.V.A.

WAR DIARY
INTELLIGENCE SUMMARY.
(Erase heading not required.)

Army Form C. 2118.

2 0

Place	Date	Hour	Summary of Events and Information	Remarks and references to Appendices
FIFE CAMP	7/10/17		Gun fired in support of 6 Third Army from 9.15 pm to 9.25 pm firing night barrage. Casualties nil.	B.M.
" "	8/10/17		Gun 1 fired for 4 minutes. Rounds fired 13,000. Very little retaliation from enemy. Casualties nil.	B.M.
" "	9/10/17		Work continued on new dug outs. Firing as per programme. Rounds expended 15,000. No 1 Section did not fire. Situation normal. Casualties nil. Work at new stables continued.	B.M.
" "	10/10/17		Firing as per programme. Rounds expended 2750. Situation normal. Casualties nil. Western front. Work on dug outs at new stables continued.	B.M.
" "	11/10/17		Firing as per programme. Situation normal. Casualties nil. Work at stables on new dug outs 6 at stables. 1 O.R. from Base Depot to transport dry interval. Firing as per programme. Rounds fired 2000. Situation normal. Casualties nil. Work at new stables continued. Wind W.	B.M.
" "	12/10/17		Nos 3 & 4 Sections relieved 1 & 2 in the line. 11 O.R. from Base Depot. reported.	222
" "	13/10/17		Firing as per programme. Rounds expended 2250. Situation normal. Casualties nil. Wind from N.N.W. Enemy aircraft active. Enemy Artillery active. 3 fair shots were obtained between the SUNKEN ROAD & the RAILWAY efforts to be made at enemy dug outs just N. from Bayard. H.Q. at m.u. of LANCER LANE. Nos One & 1 & 2 Sections moved into billets in ARRAS.	B.M.

WAR DIARY or INTELLIGENCE SUMMARY

Army Form C. 2118.

Place	Date	Hour	Summary of Events and Information	Remarks and references to Appendices
ARRAS	14/10/17		At 4.55 p.m. the guns fired in cooperation with a raid carried out by XI Division. Rapid fire for 10 minutes. Rounds expended 9500. At 9.30 p.m. guns fired again in support of raid made on our left. Rounds expended 7500 - Exhaustion and harassing with fire of various calibres to T m.g. At 2.45 p.m. an enemy aeroplane flew over our lines. Weather fine. Wind light. Work on dug outs & ablution huts continued.	S.A.A.
"	15/10/17		Guns fired according to programme. Rounds expended 1750. Situation normal. Casualties nil. Wind light. W to S.W. Work on dug outs D.R.T. and new Latrine continued.	S.A.A.
"	16/10/17		Guns fired according to programme. Rounds fired 1750. Casualties nil. Situation normal. Wind W to S.W. light. Work done necessary S.O.S. duty & mending wire cut. Transport moved to new Lodgers in ARRAS - CAMBRAI ROAD	S.A.A.
"	17/10/17		Tupple engaged in conjunction with artillery between 8 p.m. & 12 m.m. rounds expended 2200. Enemy fired with one gun during the morning in RED HOUSE DUMP (115.MAR.B??) but without damage. Guns and Shell landed in SUNKEN ROAD in front of our bow. Casualties nil. At 9.50 a.m. heavy bombardment by the artillery which lasted ? minutes. Ward Minor continuing construction of dug outs. Weather. Situation otherwise normal.	D.A.
"	18/10/17		Guns fired according to programme. Rounds fired 2000. Casualties nil. Situation normal.	S.A.A.
"	19/10/17		100,000 rations about 3 & 4 batteries in the line. I.O.R. reported from Base depot. Horses & mules were there the diff batteries on the programme. Rounds fired 1250. Situation normal. Casualties nil.	S.A.A.

WAR DIARY or INTELLIGENCE SUMMARY

Army Form C. 2118.

22

Place	Date	Hour	Summary of Events and Information	Remarks and references to Appendices
ARRAS	20/10/17		Gun fired on PELVES MILL and DELBAR WOOD during the night. Rounds expended 6000. Casualties nil. Situation normal. Work slow - softening dug-out in SUNKEN ROAD.	2/A
—	21/10/17		Two alternative frontages dug to camouflaged newly cut trampoline borrow. Cuttons out of the clearing guns. B.S.M. R/2 ASHBORNER to Command No.4 AUTEAUSSART from fire on GUNTRENCH, RIVER TRACKS & PELVES BRIDGE. Rounds expended 3000. Situation quiet - Casualties nil. Work slow continuing dug-outs.	2/A
—	22/10/17		Guns fired on fire programme. Rounds expended 4000. Casualties nil. Situation normal. Work continued on dug-outs.	2/A
—	23/10/17		Guns fired on tenth night programme in RIVER TRACKS & PELVES BRIDGE. Rounds expended 4250. Casualties nil. Enemy activity between also T.M.S. Work continued in day out.	2/A
—	24/10/17		Guns fired in support of front on B sub. in support area at 2/am. Zero hour. No.1 Battery from Zero C 2m + 10 mins + from 2m + 1h. P m h. - Zero + 1 hr 15m h. Rounds fired 2600. No. 2 Battery fired cut Zero to 2m + 2.0 m's. Zero + 7.0 E 2 + 100. Rounds fired 10,000. Casualties 2/Lt. DYRE wounded. Several thrown line. Enemy retaliation from 5mm on 6th Battery positions. Work slow, continuing dug-outs.	2/A
—	25/10/17		Guns fired on fire programme. Rounds expended 8700. Attending functions for No. 2 Battery amidst Enemy batteries near Actury. Bombed at FAMPOUX. Situation normal. Casualties nil.	2/A

A5834 Wt. W4973/M687 750,000 8/16 D. D. & L. Ltd. Forms/C.2118/13

Army Form C. 2118.

WAR DIARY
INTELLIGENCE SUMMARY.
(Erase heading not required.)

Place	Date	Hour	Summary of Events and Information	Remarks and references to Appendices
ARRAS	26/10/17		2/Lt A.J. SMITH and 2 O.R. joined from Base Depot. Sections 3 & 4 relieved Sections 1 & 2 in the line. Relief was completed by 5.15pm. Guns fired during the night as per programme. Rounds expended 1500. No 2 Battery moved to alternative position. Casualties nil.	D.A.A
~	27/10/17		Situation normal. Work done S.O.A. as per programme. Rounds expended to rear light M.G. Aerial activity nil.	C.A.A
~	28/10/17		Guns fired barrage to programme. Rounds expended 1500. Enemy shelling section heavy. No activity [illegible]. Casualties and situation normal. No S.O.A calls from infantry so not gone fired.	B.A.A
~	29/10/17		Situation normal. Casualties nil. Wore down - Reploating S.O.A. ordinary trench gun drill. Wind light SW to ESE.	
~	29/10/17		Guns fired to programme. Rounds expended 2000. Heavy bombardment of own artillery at 5.30am. Shooting Left on Item be one left. Situation otherwise normal. Casualties nil. Wire gun fire falling in Front & displaying aerial trench forwards in morning for situation to rear. 2/Lt R.I.R.X. reported from CALAIS.	C.A.A
~	30/10/17		Guns fired to programme. Rounds fired 2000. Situation normal. Casualties nil. Wire down and wiring to the N side and has No. 1 Battery experienced running wire. Total of 500. Rent meant for sections to rest.	C.A.A
~	31/10/17		2/Lt D.a. HARDING joined from Base. Guns fired to programme 2200 rounds lining adjusted. Casualties and enemy movement nil. Aerial activity. Situation otherwise normal. FAM HO.	D.A.A

Confidential

War Diary
of
225th Company, M.G. Corps.

From 1 Nov 1917 to 30 Nov 1917.

(Volume 5)

Army Form C. 2118.

WAR DIARY
INTELLIGENCE SUMMARY.
(Erase heading not required.)

Place	Date	Hour	Summary of Events and Information	Remarks and references to Appendices
ARRAS	1.11.17		M.O.R. just in from Brus. Sport. Targets were engaged by the Sections in the line as per programme, 2000 rounds being fired. During the day FAMPOUX were heavily shelled with "Heavies." Two of our 18 pdr Shells dropped short, exploding at WESTERN END of MOUNT PLEASANT WOOD. WORK DONE:- Deep Dug out continued & progress report sent to the C.R.E. Trench improvements carried on. Casualties nil. The Section out of the line carried on with drill under the Section Officer.	W.P.T.
ARRAS.	2.11.17		Targets were engaged by the Sections in the line as per programme. 2000 rounds being fired. Casualties nil. Telephone was removed from No 2 BATTERY. No1 & 2 Sections relieved No 3 & 4 Sections in the line. The relieving Sections going up by boat to FAMPOUX & the Sections relieved coming back to ARRAS by boat.	W.P.T.
ARRAS.	3.11.17		Targets were engaged by the Sections in the line as per programme. 2750 rds being fired. Situation normal. Casualties nil. WORK DONE:- Deep Dug out continued & progress report sent to C.R.E. S.A.A. stores brought up for the guns. Sections out of the line cleaned gun equipment which were inspected by Section Officer. Pay & Batt Parade were also held.	W.P.T.
ARRAS.	4.11.17		Targets were engaged by the Sections in the line as per programme, 2750 rounds being fired. At 1.45 A.M. The enemy opened a barrage on the right front of our Division. He apparently raided the S.O.S. went up. The guns of No 1 BATTERY opened fire, firing 1 belt per gun & then standing by to await developments. Nothing happened to they stood down at 2.45 AM. No 2 BATTERY did not fire.	W.P.T.

Army Form C. 2118.

WAR DIARY
or
INTELLIGENCE SUMMARY.

(Erase heading not required.)

25

Place	Date	Hour	Summary of Events and Information	Remarks and references to Appendices
ARRAS	4.11.17	Continued	No 1 BATTERY reports that their telephone to BRIGADE has been cut off. Work done. Work was continued on the deep dug-out. Casualties. Nil. The Sections out of the line attended Church Parade.	P.T.
ARRAS	5.11.17		No 2 BATTERY co-operated with Artillery in raid made by the 47th DIVISION firing from 4.30 to 5.15 P.M. Rounds fired 2250. Target DELEAR WOOD. Both BATTERIES did the usual night firing as per programme. Rounds fired 2250. During the Raid the Enemy artillery was very active paying special attention to the CHEMICAL WORKS, CHATEAU, CEYLON AVENUE, MOUNT PLEASANT WOOD, CRETE and the EMBANKMENT. These parts were all heavily shelled with heavies. The situation became normal soon after the Raid was over. Work done. The deep dug out was continued & is now nearing Completion. Progress Report sent to C.R.E. Casualties. Nil. The Sections out of the line paraded from 9 to 12 A.M. under Section Officers for Gas drill, work on the Gun & Arm drill.	P.T.
ARRAS	6.11.17		Targets were engaged by the Sections in the line as per programme. 2750 rounds was fired. Situation Normal. Casualties nil. Work was continued on the deep dug-out. The Sections out of the line paraded from 9 to 12 A.M. under Section Officers for Gas drill (men casualties fitted No 8 S.B.Rs by Divisional Gas N.C.O.) Arm drill work on the Gun.	M.T.S.

Pte DAVIDSON No 21825 was tried by Field General Court-martial.

A5834 Wt.W4973/M687 750,000 8/16 D.D.&L.Ltd. Forms/C.2118/13

Army Form C. 2118.

26

WAR DIARY
or
INTELLIGENCE SUMMARY.
(Erase heading not required.)

Place	Date	Hour	Summary of Events and Information	Remarks and references to Appendices
ARRAS.	7.11.17		Targets were engaged by Nos. 1 & 2 Batteries as per programme. 3000 rounds being fired. Situation normal. Casualties nil. Work was continued on the deep dugout, also a wooden frame was fixed into one of the alternative positions. No sections out of the line paraded from 9 to 12 AM for Bell-filling & preparing the fuses for the line.	M.M.
ARRAS.	8.11.17		Targets engaged by No. 2 Battery as per programme. 1250 rounds being fired. No. 1 Battery did not fire owing to all the necessary preparations for the raid & going through tunnels & roads. Situation normal. Casualties nil. Work was carried on in the deep dugout & all the necessary arrangements were completed for the raid. The 3 sections out of the line paraded for Gas drill & Shell filling from 9.15 to 12 AM.	M.M.
ARRAS	9.11.17 9.15 pm 1.40 am		Sentence was received the late DAVIDSON No. 22828 & he was informed of this at a Company parade. The sentence being 91 days F.P. No 1. 50 days of which were remitted. Enemy barraged our two forward T.M. T. Heavy trestles ones CHEMICAL WORKS & RIVER SCARPE also ones from CURB SWITCH TRENCH fired in support of a raid carried out by the 46" Inf. Bde on the enemy trench. Rounds Expended 24,750. Casualties nil. Enemy was to 25 mins according to programme. Rumour from enemy we lost a number to enemy by 5 am then from FAMPOUX. Little retaliation from the enemy. No. 3 Section returned No. 1 Section in the line. Work continued in dugout, they met in the SUNKEN ROAD. Harassing fire carried on as per programme. Ammn fd. 22500.	M.M.

WAR DIARY
INTELLIGENCE SUMMARY.
(Erase heading not required.)

Army Form C. 2118.

Place	Date	Hour	Summary of Events and Information	Remarks and references to Appendices
ARRAS	10.11.17	4.45 am	No. 4 Section relieved No. 2 Section in the line. Enemy lightly bombarded CORDITE, CORFU, CRETE & CEYLON Trenches with H.E. also (Factory H.42). This was continued until 6.50 a.m. Again from 8-9 am & from 9.30-10 am. Our S.A.A. Bty. & Trench Mortars did no Large. Approximately 100 shells were fired from Coventwerfen. No. 2 Bty. did not fire. No. 1 Bty. fired on PELVES MILL RUINED TRACK & to PELVES BRIDGE & CROSS ROADS — 1000 rounds being expended. Enemy aeroplane to east from on DELBAR WOOD & HAUSA WOOD. No. 1 Section claiming guns & ticks & victims up to afternoon. Guns fired by programme, rounds expended 2,900.	PW
"	11.11.17	3.30 am	Enemy bombarded our artillery positions with gas shells — there was just mist in Large numbers for about an hour. Own Batteries stood to, with gas masks on but 5 pm. Wore day & of on to forward Rd Sparsely shelled. Batty. Relief taken to Bde. Both relieved. Normal amount of Generation and Extraction Ostriches movement. Wind light W. Trench flooded for beling in mat.	PW
"	12.11.17	9.10 am	Guns fired according to programme — rounds expended 2,000. Enemy appear just from gas shells on our artillery positions. Batteries attempt to wait for wash on. Situation otherwise normal. Character not four Q own aeroplane flying very low first on enemy trenches then those containing deep dug outs in SUNKEN ROAD	PW

Army Form C. 2118.

28

WAR DIARY
INTELLIGENCE SUMMARY
(Erase heading not required.)

Place	Date	Hour	Summary of Events and Information	Remarks and references to Appendices
ARRAS	13.11.17		Guns of No 1 Bty fired as per programme, rounds expended 1000. Guns of No 2 Bty were not ready to carry out practice at dusk. Telescope sights did not fire. Cartridges not yet received. Return at last received in batt. Getting ready for intensive shoot.	MM
—	14.11.17		Guns fired as per intensive programme, rounds expended 14,000. The need by to 45° Infantry Bde was cancelled owing to bad weather. Intensive situation otherwise as with like Cartridges and returns as per practical consolidation of shell hole.	MM
—	15.11.17	5 am	A trench was dug up with ammunition to No 2. Bty. occupying in SINGLE ARCH for No 1 Bty. Gun fired as per intensive programme - rounds expended 11,000.	MM
		5.30 pm	at 5.30 pm enemy put down an extremely violent barrage. Apparently in retaliation to a raid being made by the 6/31 Bn. The enemy worked the area CEYLON - CORPS & RLY EMBKT SINGLE ARCH RD & FAMPOOX CHINSTRAP LANE On shell fell on corner of our new dug out in SUNKEN ROAD. Our 9 pm situation again was normal. Casualties nil. Work done Bulk (?) with taken to fire position trench of S.A.A. for up. Return in as went for 6 rounds rapid	
			from every alternate with type target mountings. Returns 1 + 2 received No 3 & 4 in the how - may being carried out by trend.	
—	16.11.17		2/Lt SMITH & HARDING returned to the Base Depot (CAMIERS). Guns fired as per intensity programme, rounds expended 2H.500 CORDITE + CORFO Timber was being brought in between 8.55 pm & 9.15 pm. Between 4.5.6 am & 5.30 am No 2. Bty were heavily shelled. Casualties nil.	MM

A 334. Wt.W4973/M687. 750,000 8/16 D.D.&L. Ltd. Forms/C.2118/13

WAR DIARY
or
INTELLIGENCE SUMMARY.

Army Form C. 2118.

29

Place	Date	Hour	Summary of Events and Information	Remarks and references to Appendices
ARRAS	17.11.17	6 a.m.	Trench mortars H.E. to SINGLE ARCH with ammunition (in No 2 Bg. 2/Lt ASHBURNER interned from XVII Corps Lt School guns fired in support of raid by 11th/12th Highr. Rounds fired 20,000. Harassing fire carried out to programme After the raid the enemy heavily shelled CORFU, CRETE, CEYLON Trenches & MT PLEASANT WOOD casualties nil. Took down half pulley amming rounds dugouts new emplacements removing ammunition from CORDITE	M
"	18.11.17		Capt FORESTER returned from leave	
		3 p.m.	Artillery trench bombardment. Both batteries fired in support on targets on fixed programme Enemy retaliated with rifle & artillery	J J
		6 p.m.	Our Infm. fire on fresh targets in support of raid by 13th /120th A.G. SCOTS During the night harassing fire was maintained on targets on programme	
		2-45 a.m.	61st DIV" raided enemy trenches. Enemy fire down a barrage in reply Total rounds fired 26,500.	
			Enemy artillery & aircraft more active than usual Enemy artillery & aircraft erected in JUNIZER ROAD on response of Pte WHITE ESSEX REGT at CRPO who was erected by 6th CAMERON H'DRS	
"	19.11.17	7-15 p.m.	Raid by 6th CAMERON H'DRS } Guns fired on new targets in support of these Enemy retaliated with rifles & heavy Gas and artillery bombardment the Gloucesters to the GLOUCESTERS & us in CORDITE	J J
		3 a.m.	Smoke and artillery barrage } artillery causing casualties to the GLOUCESTERS & us in CORDITE	
		6.20 a.m.	and CORFU Harassing fire was carried out in the night as ordered Artillery activity fairly vigorous on both sides. A dump of ammo was fired near CHEMICAL WORKS which were heavily shelled as also FAMPOUX (Dainty Jess)	

Army Form C. 2118.

30

WAR DIARY
or
INTELLIGENCE SUMMARY.
(Erase heading not required.)

Place	Date	Hour	Summary of Events and Information	Remarks and references to Appendices
ARRAS	19.11.17	1pm	184th INFY BDE carried out a raid	J.J.
			90906 PTE ELLIS H.S. killed by H.E. shell	
			Total rounds fired 22,500	
"	20.11.17	11.30 a.m.	90906 PTE ELLIS H.S. buried by Revd. W.L. ARROWSMITH, 9th the 184th Infy Bde. in BROWN'S COPSE CEMETERY. CAPTN ALLEN and DRVR GRACIE proceeded on leave	
			During the day various targets were engaged by both batteries firing at the rate of 5 to 10 per hour by night.	
		6pm	1000 rds was fired (harassing fire)	
			Sections 3 & 4 went up to maintain the continued Divl Rnds, firing two 6 gun batteries	1/J
			Guns fired in support of advance. Divl Reinf. for 24 hours after which the Bn's mentioned	
		6 a.m.	M & N4 Batteries	
		3 a.m.	Enemy opened heavy bombardment of front trenches being by T M's and artillery & guns at	
		4-4:30 a.m. to 5:30 a.m.		
			Positions were reconnoitred from ... ... was no advance.	
			Rounds fired 26,500.	
			Artillery was more active on both sides. The enemy apparently being all out long range. Rds. fired 2500	
"	21.11.17		Normal harassing fire was resumed. No enemy trench tkoucroaks.	
		9 pm	Raid by OUR OWN on Left	J.J.
			Artillery on both sides more active than usual	
			hostile TM & MG activity.	
			Aeroplanes. Our own fairly active - enemy's guns hit and observation balloon up. Visibility poor	
			Best patls. arrived on. 1 captive ballon seen to Left. Rds. Dump Bww notified returned.	
			116200 PTE CATLING wounded above knee by H.E. shell.	

WAR DIARY or INTELLIGENCE SUMMARY

Army Form C. 2118.

Place	Date	Hour	Summary of Events and Information	Remarks and references to Appendices
ARRAS	22-11-17	5 a.m.	Hostile harassing fire was directed on enemy roads Butler Trench. Fire was opened in cooperation with discharge of gas in CHALK PIT and surrounding area. Rounds fired 3,250. Our artillery was normal. Enemy intermittently active. T.M. quiet. Our aeroplanes whilst active, shewed they were hemmed in two E.A. fire-barriers one here in the morning. P&Os were fired upon. Our A.A. not off. duty, motivated in use of Shrouds, however shell + Tau Ross. NCO's instructed in importance of machine directly of plane. The new crew of the bed returned expensive cracks Aerial type drill.	J.J.
"	23-11-17		Harrassing fire carried out by No. 1 Battery. Rds fired 1000. Enemy + our artillery active, also aeroplanes. Situation normal. No. 4 Sect. began their EMBANKMENT to CRUMP TRENCH.	J.J.
"	24-11-17		Both Batteries stood to' during night in readiness for C.O.'s shot, on hostile harassing fire, owing to advice recd that enemy appeared to be massing on our front, and an attack was expected. Nothing happened. Our artillery was active, paying special attention to PLOUVAIN. Enemy quiet. No aeroplanes owing to left mist + low clouds.	J.J.
"	25-11-17		Harrassing fire a usual subjects during night. Rds fired 2500. Situation normal and artillery + aeroplanes quiet. Day quiet except enemy active. Section at H.Q. Lp. – action drill harnessed up + T.P.T.	J.J.
"	26-11-17	2 p.m.	Usual harassing fire continued during night on enemy crossroads etc. Rds fired 3,500. ROEUX, CHEMICAL WORKS + CORPU AVENUE hearily shelled for 30 mins. Our artillery very active also enemy aeroplanes. Aeroplane active + recalled favourable object pointed to hostile approach. Sect at H.Q. T.P.T. action drill removed is. this impedein	J.J.

WAR DIARY or INTELLIGENCE SUMMARY

Army Form C. 2118.

32

Place	Date	Hour	Summary of Events and Information	Remarks and references to Appendices
ARRAS	27-11-17		Usual harassing fire carried out from dusk to midnight. Rds fired 3,500. Both artilleries intermittently active. Situation normal.	V.J
"	28-11-17		Preparations made for relief. Sections in ARRAS. Two Offrs & 1.A. Section in ARRAS. Two sick & 1.A. As the 16th DIVN was taken over the front of the 61st DIVN which was being put out, we relieved 8 guns of 184 M.G. Coy & 8 guns of 183 M.G. Coy. The former handed in to us COPPER TRENCH and the latter in a small trench off CHILI TRENCH. The relief was only carried out during the day & the guns were laid on their S.O.S. lines. Belts were taken over from both Coys, also bipods from 183 Coy. The necessary papers were handed over to two Serjts. also where ammy. F.O.B.	V.J
"	29-11-17		No firing was done. The trench being opened on having gone 4 only when ammy F.O.B. Artillery on both sides were intermittently active. M.Gs & T.Ms were quiet. Aerial activity normal. Rds fired 4,250. Harassing fire resumed from our positions. Enemy artillery very active. Barrage put down on our left twice. Enemy attempted but stopped before reaching our lines. Our men stood to but were not needed. Two enemy aeroplanes came over our line. North & Hy. battery being informed. Sects. at H.Q.s. P.T. Manual. ARRAS shelled fairly freely. Three Officers killed V.J. No harassing fire by others.	V.J
"	30-11-17	1-30pm	No destructive shoot to carry to enemy bombardment but nothing happened. things quietened down about 1.30pm. Relief of Sections 3rd by Sects 1 + 2 aptly completed by 4pm. After artillery activity in the morning the enemy indirectly quietened & things were normal in respect of M.Gs T.Ms & airplanes. ARRAS shelled by H.V. gun.	V.J

Vol 6

Confidential

War Diary
of
225th Coy. M. G. Corps

from 1st December 1917 to 31st December, 1917.

(Volume 6)

Army Form C. 2118.

33

WAR DIARY
or
INTELLIGENCE SUMMARY.
(Erase heading not required.)

Instructions regarding War Diaries and Intelligence Summaries are contained in F.S. Regs., Part II. and the Staff Manual respectively. Title pages will be prepared in manuscript.

Place	Date	Hour	Summary of Events and Information	Remarks and references to Appendices
ARRAS	1-12-17		"B" Battery fired 1780 rds. harassing fire. A Hun airplane shelled our front line. Men were given showers in "Shandy". Kept very quietly in decoration for various trips. Enemy artillery intermittantly active. Our guns quiet. Some aeroplane activity. Trenches full, positions unformed. Much cleaned. 2/Lt. LUNN joined the Bn. from X'mas.	
"	2-12-17		Harrassing fire resumed on enemy H.Q. area. Rds fired 5,000. Artillery on both sides quieter. Aeroplanes more active owing to better visibility. "B" Battery had an infantry working party under R.E.s. improving forward trenches, employed during night by section.	
"	3-12-17		Harrassing fire carried on resumed on enemy's tracks. Reverting to Rds fired 5,500. Artillery T.Ms & M.Gs on both sides quieter than usual. Aeroplanes more active as visibility was poor. 2/Lt. LUNN posted to Keen I, went up to his section. Practice spouts - 6" were had, & trenches were nearly improved at 22.825 PTE DAVIDSON.T who was employed (FP No 1) wounded in nose when the fire hissed on the firing room. No evidence known him to signs of there. No casualties among the dinner out on Aeroplat. PTE Ho trenches of enemy Rd fire scarcely. Usual harrassing fire. On our right he shelled the CEMETERY heavily, also CHEMICAL WORKS heavily with large shells from 8-3 a.m. to 4 a.m.	
"	4-12-17	9 p.m. 2-45 a.m. 5-30 a.m.	to CHEMICAL WORKS heavily round FAMPOUX also artillery positions near Our men return to near "B" Bn Murdock. Gas shells round FAMPOUX no rds used Aircraft. Our active. Enemy unusually active. One E.A. reported shells down to tree line Nowering. Aeroplanes... up as visibility not very good. T.Ms L.Ms G.Ss quiet. Casualties 4636 Pte BETTS wounded Kemmel shrapnel by a piece & A.A shrapnel	

WAR DIARY
or
INTELLIGENCE SUMMARY.

Army Form C. 2118.

B 4

Place	Date	Hour	Summary of Events and Information	Remarks and references to Appendices
ARRAS	5-12-17	6.p.m.	Harassing fire carried out against Ref. trench 4.2.50. Practise trenches carried out. After a quiet day for artillery, ours became active & visits great effect to the enemy's wire.	
			Our lock stand "B" but was not received.	
		10 p.m.	Enemy abandoned posts of NORTHY	
		10-15 p.m.	on left of our position	
			T. M. Gs quiet. Enemy's M.Gs. active.	
			Sniper's fire very active. One of ours was hung back in our lines. Numerous enemy snipers reported in front of	
		10-30 p.m	Some two sent over but not enough or not near enough to incommode hostile return	
			Work carried on in the temporary engineering franchise at Ref. point 4.2.50 Reference 27 Millimetre ?	
			Day quiet.	
			Summary of evidence taken by CAPTN FORESTER in the case of 25243 Pte I. CLARK [?] during absent	
			without leave.	
"	6-12-17		H.00 p.m. Fired during harassing fire. Artillery normal T.M.S. & M.Gs rather more active.	
			Aircraft very active owing to fine visibility in morning.	
			Work to trench of "B" battery continued & ordinary work carried on. Relieve at HQ & usual check	
			taken as per supplementary Ref. point 4.2.50	
"	7-12-17		Artillery. One a/c over that's active. Enemy's quiet.	
			Aircraft. Five of our planes flew over enemy lines between 3 & 4 ship.. long burst Ack Ack fire	
			They were heavily engaged by E.A.A. but all got safely over our lines Carols to by 3-30 p.m.	
"	8-12-17		Relief of "B" section completed by 3-30 p.m. Artillery quiet. Fired a few rounds harassing	
			4.2.50 pub. fired. Enemy fired Harassing fire on MURCAY area. E.M. Gs fairly active, sweeping neighbourhood of both our T.M. garrison & Little exception activity on enemy front. Our Lewis active in sweeping their.. line.	
			Our enemy prisoner reported escaped & at large near "B" battery. No anything seen [?]	

Army Form C. 2118.

WAR DIARY
or
INTELLIGENCE SUMMARY.

(Erase heading not required.)

Instructions regarding War Diaries and Intelligence Summaries are contained in F.S. Regs., Part II. and the Staff Manual respectively. Title pages will be prepared in manuscript.

Place	Date	Hour	Summary of Events and Information	Remarks and references to Appendices
ARRAS	9-12-17		No harassing fire or special orders received. In the particulars on the wire & other were laid on S.O.S. lines in anticipation of an attack which was developed & destroyed. Service wire from 5 a.m. to 8-30 a.m. when normale tournedre was resumed. During the day 2/Lt G.M.M. Mead & 3 O.R.s to appear "B" battery. Pte CRAIGIE sent down from line sick & for internal shelling normal. Enemy quiet on 9-12-17 but active early on 10-12-17. E.A. Flyers been two own lines apparently	J.S.
"	10/12/17		two twin clean sight company fired single shots & longs fire in reply them to artillery made observe. Pten two deer night light. Artillery, Ours normal. Enemy active, his wire with considerable accuracy night & day. HENDECOURT & CHERISY/RIENCOURT-LEZ-PREUX position. A few arrived & intermittent special attention to CHERISY. Ours normal. Enemy very active from & 10 E.A. came up to our fire dropt. Averaged two normal. Enemy very active. No aerial fights observed. up not hoopd. Enemy reinforcing very active & tried to bomb 6 app. but left as the town was defended. Casualty 67905 Pte FENNER (wounded) left arm, shell through the ankle & knee Rifle Brigade at John Roger	J.S.
"	11/12/17		59391 Pte SHEPPARD cut down & passed in train Transport for ammunition went to Fast 3. I'm putting also ammunition & Sunny rode 8 ammunition followed up. Rachisses fire many & some fresh shells 5 miles only & settle & easy fire many to advance On for 600 shrinking any quick shots but 2 & 3 of arts were being away fire only to continue. Artillery, Ours very active from 8-15 - 9-30 for No new any pen. Enemy quiet & alone. He appears very 2 occupy	J.S.
"	12/12/17		SNIRPS Retalation ... Enemy quiet & alone in his retaliation to put 6-30 for. The enemy strong along & town 6-10 Loss in a group of 5 but the previous to when out 4 same at away to see Loss in a group of 6-10 but he E.A. opie flies very low over our lines. It was normal for E.A. opie flies very low over our lines. In ARRAS during the day 3 have been dropping shells with special attention to the Station. Pattern Deaths. Corps Commander visited Batteries	J.S.

A 5834 Wt.W.4973/M.687 750,000 8/16 D.D.&L. Ltd. Forms/C.2118/13.

Army Form C. 2118.

36

WAR DIARY
or
INTELLIGENCE SUMMARY.
(Erase heading not required.)

Instructions regarding War Diaries and Intelligence Summaries are contained in F. S. Regs., Part II. and the Staff Manual respectively. Title pages will be prepared in manuscript.

Place	Date	Hour	Summary of Events and Information	Remarks and references to Appendices
ARRAS	13/12/17		No hostile fire as observed. Patrols to our own wire. No casualties. Enemy's rear lines. Artillery etc normal throughout night. Hospital.	
"	14/12/17		Nos 1 & 2 Batteries fired 3 & 4 on the line B Bty fired during the night 1500 rounds during barrage. At 2 p.m. enemy heavily bombarded our front line with T.M. when stood to. Our Artillery retaliated sharply. Casualties nil. W.R. continued to harass frog & B Bty.	
"	15/12/17		Guns fired during night - rounds reported 3000 Christmas mistletoe which is both sides. Artillery active. Casualties nil. Wire returned and camouflage.	
"	16/12/17		Guns fired during the night 3800 rounds approx M.G. Situation normal. Casualties nil. Capt. FORESTER returned a forward H.Q. in the trenches.	
"	17/12/17		Lt. P. CLARKE was killed by F.O.O. in at 10" stn. Am Col McLarens at. his was wounded slightly. A Bty, B Bty fired to harass M&V. Rounds reported 3000 Situation normal Casualties nil	
"	18/12/17	9 a.m. to 4.45 p.m.	Guns fired during night 6000 rounds. Army retaliated. Enemy heavily bombarded our front. Heavens shots with fire a little fired from battery. There were times of gun which fired to 3 gun battery position between firing & CAMEL AVENUE. Guns and handles affected our shoots in CRIME Return afford a little. 4 T & 5 Men units guns medium am Arml (our to the enemy). Very active. Casualties nil. Field front	
"	19/12/17		Guns fired during night - rounds reported 4700 normal artillery & T.M. activity. Casualties nil. Weather very cold & frosty.	

WAR DIARY
or
INTELLIGENCE SUMMARY.

(Erase heading not required.)

Army Form C. 2118.

Instructions regarding War Diaries and Intelligence Summaries are contained in F. S. Regs., Part II. and the Staff Manual respectively. Title pages will be prepared in manuscript.

37

Place	Date	Hour	Summary of Events and Information	Remarks and references to Appendices
ARRAS	20/12/17		Guns fired during night - rounds expended 7500. Retaliation against Germans not heavy on enemy's continued. Situation quiet during night Grippi gun man hipi recovered & find about [illeg]	277
"	21/12/17		Guns fired during night - rounds expended 2000. Situation Normal. Casualties nil 9 T.M. Batteries retired Return 1 & 2 in the line	277
"	22/12/17		Guns fired during night - rounds expended 5500 Situation normal Troops N. A of SCARPE. One prisoner retaken who came forward from our right of the SCARPE. Guns dead down by 6.45 am. 60 cells [illeg]	277
"	23/12/17		Guns [illeg] at 5,000 rounds. Enemy activity very active - main attack to [illeg] from A.M. - 6.30pm. Course except [illeg] that many [illeg] Columns of Wanton and [illeg]	322
"	24/12/17 6.30pm		Enemy [illeg] down a heavy bombardment on our right at 6.30pm. S.O.S. sent up B. Battery opened fire in support By 7.15pm all was quiet. Rounds fired 500 Enemy heavily [illeg] MONCHY. Casualties nil. It is not clear who replaced to open fire B. Battery, guns [illeg] round to [illeg] "Lt. CLARKE sent to N° 3 [illeg] Staff Hospital at DOULLENS for treatment to his mounted [illeg] 2/22 92 2 ? [illeg]	277
"	26/12/17		Went recently free carried out 4,000 also heavy fire everything very quiet 8/800 [illeg] Left guns G.T. T. & 12 [illeg] 3. Gode life on the programme. Enemy TM's active at times every now and then heavy 1st [illeg] New army trucks used one for observed fire of B. Batty. Couples taken [illeg] to performance	
"	27/12/17		appeared him present from minor fire [illeg] normal. [illeg] Lewis 6,500 100 fired. Luners nev Dr. Enemy casualty [illeg] about B. Batty's work [illeg]	
"	28/12/17			

WAR DIARY or INTELLIGENCE SUMMARY

Army Form C. 2118.

Place	Date	Hour	Summary of Events and Information	Remarks and references to Appendices
ARRAS	28/12/17		Relief of Sectors 3 and 4 completed by Nos. 1 & 2 Bys at 8 am 28/12/17. Enemy artillery active especially round FAMPOUX. E.A. active. Other Bys quiet. Bomb dropped near our HQ.	
"	30/12/17		6,250 rds harassing fire on Bosch areas during night. Normal activity.	
"	31/12/17		7,800 rds expended on harassing fire and intermittent activity. Enemy activity normal.	
"	1/1/18		2 p.m. All Gunner went to Camp Centre night 31/12 – 1/1.	
			2.15 MG Bdy Order No 8	
			Ref Mss 378 HW Pozzo Signed Mao H 9000	
			1. A & B Bys 225 M Coy will relieve on the night of 3/4 July 2/3 Coy by	
			2. No. 1 Section detachment of Medium Guns will be the two on the night 2/3 Jany.	
			Two Medium MGs will be in CAM VALLEY (A15,30 b 05) and suffix.	
			3 (a) All Batty Comd officers will familiarise themselves	
			(b) Team Leader will note belts to be assembled, range cards & barrage instructions	
			4. Parades will be all carried out	
			Separate instructions have already been issued re relief the Machine Guns of	
			advanced HQ Bn Group	
			5. Reports on reliefs have been sent in pursuing arrangements of Sectors	
			6. On completion of relief reports will have been Bn Group Officers with the Bn de Corps 178g	
			7. The completion of relief will be reported by use G. - 1 Coy Reserve. 2 OMGO 15.12.18	
			Name of the code word RUGBY	
			J. Forrest Capt, adj H.S.G.	
"	20/1/18		Issued as at 10 a.m. 31/12/17 Rangefinders	
			Capm? - 1. 4"F. Bdr, Dec. 2, 46's b. - 6, dir 2. 15" H.Q. vA. + OMGO ISHm. E. OMGO HW Stagg	
			and with Bdr of H.Q. M Captain B Officer M Captain G Van Bury	
			Complete relieve with Bn G.H.Q prepared from VM under E.H.A. BARLOW and 2/Lt. H.W. STAGG	

Confidential

War Diary
of
225th M.G. Company

from 1st January 1918 to 31st Jany 1918.

(Volume 7)

WAR DIARY or INTELLIGENCE SUMMARY

Army Form C. 2118.

Place	Date	Hour	Summary of Events and Information	Remarks and references to Appendices
ARRAS	1/1/19		Corps sites inspected in known area. Lieut. Charlton arrived & everything quiet in S.A. area down near A HQ's in FAMPOUX. Officers & NCO's look well.	
		22.5	M.G. Coy Order No 9. Ref. Map 57.B 1/40,000	
			1. The 19th R.D. ... [illegible] ... will be maintained on the Repos Reserve.	
			2. The 22.5 M.G.C. will move its head-qrs at DAINVILLE in the Arras area 2.1.19 [illegible]	
			1919 4 A Platoon - ARRAS - DAINVILLE.	
			3. An officer & one party will reconnoitre the new Repos area.	
			4. The [illegible] party under 2/Lt PETERKIN will [illegible] all available men when quiet on the line. The [illegible] guns with carriages [illegible] and parts Coy 2nd will [illegible]	
			5. The first party will provide one advance billet in area to [illegible]	
			6. The transport will be drawn up to the Rue de L'ANCIEN RIVAGE [illegible] heads turned to the PLACE DE COCLIPAS	
			7. The second party will move at 11 am on January 2nd 1919. Order 40 fg & 4 inf	
			8. In event of return not [illegible] by first party	
			9. An advance billeting party will proceed ahead of the main body [illegible]	
			[illegible] orders have been issued.	
			[signature] J. [illegible] Capt.	
			22 - M.G.C.	

Issued at [illegible]
Copies 1, 2 M.G.B, 2, 4th D.H.Q. 3 File 2 Fair Diary

Army Form C. 2118.

WAR DIARY
or
INTELLIGENCE SUMMARY.
(Erase heading not required.)

Instructions regarding War Diaries and Intelligence Summaries are contained in F. S. Regs., Part II. and the Staff Manual respectively. Title pages will be prepared in manuscript.

40

Place	Date	Hour	Summary of Events and Information	Remarks and references to Appendices
ARRAS	2/1/18		Nos 3 + 4 Sections left Billets in ARRAS & marched to DAINVILLE for rest	2.2
			Nos 1 + 2 Sections arrived in line by M.G. GUARDS & spent night in billets in ARRAS	
DAINVILLE	3/1/18		Nos 1 + 2 Sections marched to DAINVILLE. 2/Lt FIELD returned from toc course	B.2
	4/1/18		Settling down in new quarters. Checking deficiencies at 2/Lt PETERKIN proceeded on leave	
	5/1/18		2.O.R transferred to 45th M.G. Coy. T 4 O.R transferred to 114 M.G. Coy	B.2
	6/1/18		Resting	
	7/1/18		Coy football to tournament Commanders Instruction	B/2
	8/1/18		The Coy (including transport) inspected by Divisional Commander. Heavy fall of snow	B/2
	9/1/18		Coy training. 2/Lt LONN proceeded to HAUTE AVESNES for 2nd course	B/2
	10/1/18		Coy training. 2.O.R transferred to 45th M.G. Coy.	B/2
	11/1/18		Coy training	B/2
	12/1/18		Coy training	B/2
	13/1/18		Resting	B/2
	14/1/18		Coy training	B/2
	15/1/18		Coy training	B/2
	16/1/18		Coy training. route march with transport. 2/Lt. ASHBURNER returned from leave	B/2
	17/1/18		Coy training. 3.O.R transferred to 44th M.G. Coy. 2.O.R transferred to 45 M.G.C	2.2
			T.I.D R & H.M.E.C.	P/2
	18/1/18		Coy training. 2/Lt FIELD proceeded on leave.	O/2
	19/1/18		Coy on MOAT Range all day. Firing Pet I G.M.G course. Also revolver practice	
	20/1/18		Resting - 2/Lt PETERKIN returned from leave	

WAR DIARY
or
INTELLIGENCE SUMMARY.

(Erase heading not required.)

Army Form C. 2118.

Place	Date	Hour	Summary of Events and Information	Remarks and references to Appendices
DAINVILLE	21/1/18		2 Sections on Divisional Range (BLANGY) 2 Sections Coy Training. Coy Commander reconnoitred gun positions for field day with 46⁰/3⁰ Bde.	
	22/1/18		Section & Sub Section Officers reconnoitred gun positions in Corps line. Coy Commander reconnoitred gun positions for field day with 2/6 & 2/6 Bde Coy on fatigue - Officers and Sub-Section reconnoitred training.	
	23/1/18		Coy Training - Afternoon all officers (except newly joined) reconnoitred ground for Bde scheme with 2/2 & 2/3 Bn. (B Reserve to A.S. Coy)	
	24/1/18		Coy Training - Afternoon football	
	25/1/18		Coy took part in Bde scheme with 46" Inf Bde. Left billets at 7.45 am returning at 2.30 pm	
	26/1/18		Coy took part in 48° Inf Bde scheme Left billets at 6.30 am returning at 3 pm	
	27/1/18		Church Parade. Coy training. Transport inspected	
	28/1/18		Coy took part in 46" Inf Bde scheme - Lewis Gun drills. Left billets at 7.45 am. Training at 2.15 pm 2/Lt FINNIGAN proceeded on leave	
	29/1/18			
	30/1/18		Coy training - Afternoon football	
	31/1/18		Coy training - Afternoon football	

CONFIDENTIAL

War Diary
of
225th Coy. M.G. Corps.

From 1st Feb 1918 to 28th Feb 1918

(Volume 8)

WAR DIARY
or
INTELLIGENCE SUMMARY.

(Erase heading not required.)

Army Form C. 2118.

Place	Date	Hour	Summary of Events and Information	Remarks and references to Appendices
DAINVILLE	1/2/18		Coy training. 57227 Sjt WEEDEN joined Coy from 15th Gen Hosp. Base Bn	
"	2/2/18		Pte HULL rejoined Coy from leave.	
"	3/2/18		Coy training. 2/Lt FIELD granted 7 days extension of leave	
"	4/2/18		CSM ROGERS rejoined Coy from 2Lyth Army Inf School.	
"	5/2/18		Coy Coy moved to near nr ARRAS. Capt E.V. Allen granted 14 days special leave to U.K. Coy arrived & now quartered in ARRAS. No. 3 Section proceeded into the line - 65/174 PG FELLOWS 14 hours to U.R.	
ARRAS	6/2/18		No. 4 Section proceeded into the line. Remainder carrying stores in new defences. 58/D5 PG ROUGHT rejoined Coy from leave No. 3 Sec stoning day and night. 45 M.O.C. Ukranian rely	
"	7/2/18	3.45 am	Enemy active. S.O.S went up on 3rd Divn front. Own fire tacken about 10 Mn . 142 between building went walks nr Scanlin. COMS KINGDOME 14 days leave to U.K.	
"	8/2/18	4.15 am	Increased enemy arm activity. Enemy put 5 trench mortar barrage on our front line. S.O.P went up from Hunms about 10 - 11 4.50 am all was quiet. Remainder of coy on Station building work Sjt STANLEY rejoined coy from W to School CAMIERS	
"	9/2/18		Situation normal. Casualties nil. K Pow taken down by No. 3 Section. 2/Lt SPRAGG + Sjt McDILL & fourth Army Inf School. Capt T FORESTER & 46th Squadron R.F.C. Situation normal.	
"	10/2/18	4 pm m.Soly	Enemy shelled the battalion to the left of FOSSES FARM & the CAMBRAI ROAD heavily Casualties nil Situation normal. 428945 Pte CALLAGHAN reported coy from 10th Infantry Corpse	

Army Form C. 2118.

43

WAR DIARY
or
INTELLIGENCE SUMMARY.
(Erase heading not required.)

Place	Date	Hour	Summary of Events and Information	Remarks and references to Appendices
ARRAS	10/2/18		Situation normal on his Internmittent shelling on both sides. Burns S.A.A. oil etc. sent of him. Situation H.mnt building until no Station Lt BARLOW left for P.T.&T course M.S. Pol. M059 Pte CLARK C to 111th Signal course 8552 Cpl WOOD T apptd 2/5/y from 25/1/18. m/s Lt ANDREWS L U.K. Capt. Allen reported by from leave.	G.R.O
"	11/2/18		3rd Lt Subburn relieved by 1/42 Battn. Situation normal. Enemy about FOSSES FARM. Incremed own activity by both sides. Capt. T FORESTER	G.R.O
"	12/2/18		Enemy shelled FOSSES FARM. Situation normal. Canadian working party relief activity in CORPS LINE. Situation at war building writes as December 2/Lt FINIGAN from leave P2596 Pte THACKERAY 14 days leave to U.K. 2/Lt LUNN & Cpl WOOD T reported Corps from XVII Corps Sig. School.	G.R.O
"	14/2/18		Increased enemy artillery activity. Situation otherwise normal. 2/Lt LUNN & FINNIGAN proceeded to hrs. 2/Lt ASHBURNER came down to Sig HQ forth interviewed on M.G. Employment in CORPS line. Work to in-int wires at Stacks continues.	G.R.O
"	15/2/18	5 am	Artillery activity on both sides. Enemy sent over a few active. Situation bombardment by enemy on own left front. Work continued in CORPS line. 60151 Cpl BAXTER L M.G. Course CAMIERS.	G.R.O
"	16/2/18		Cpl Stocke 26066 2/Cpl FARMERY 14 days leave to U.K. 2/Cpl PARKES reported to from leave. During the day own A.A. fire nr SP.T.R. POSTS engaged enemy aircraft - apparently information to to work continued on M.G emplacements in 3rd System. Enemy himself shelled neighbourhood of FOSSES FARM. Considerable Air Activity on both sides.	G.R.O
	3-4pm			

A 5834 Wt. W 4973/M687 750,000 8/16 D.D. & L. Ltd. Forms/C.2118/13

Army Form C. 2118.

WAR DIARY
or
INTELLIGENCE SUMMARY.

(Erase heading not required.)

Place	Date	Hour	Summary of Events and Information	Remarks and references to Appendices
ARRAS	17/2/18		Our A.A. gun at R Pier engaged E.A. Enemy aircraft during the day. Ammunition expended 10/15rds. Enemy artillery active about FOSSES FARM – QUALLY Enemy sent over two shells bearing enemy uniform. Situation otherwise unchanged.	
"	18/2/18	10pm	Situation generally quiet. Artillery activity increasing on both sides. WWA works on 3rd system improvements. Weather dull turning to showers. Casualties nil	
"	19/2/18		3rd & 4th Echelon relieved 1 & 2 Echelons in the Battery Positions on both main WWA continued on 3rd System. Casualties nil	
"	20/2/18		Situation generally quiet. Enemy sent over a few 77 shells. Enemy m/g active W/. Renewed	
"	21/2/18		Situation generally quiet. Enemy shelled Burrow Lodge V.1. Rest cont on WWA on 3rd System. Work continued on improvements. Casualties nil	
"	22/2/18	3am	Own guns co-operated by artillery fire. A great much hostile A.A. M.G M.G on enemy lines. Rounds expended 11,000. Enemy also in retaliating. By 4.30am our fire had died on 14 Army Area. A.B.O. found from Shot Posts. Situation generally quiet. Intermittent shelling on both sides. Counter battery work	
"	23/2/18		continued on 3rd System improvements.	
"	24/2/18		Normal artillery on M. G. activity on both sides. Our A.A. guns on A fire & 50 fired 30 & 250 rounds respectively in many attempts on enemy aircraft H ETRUN. In course of aeroplane photograph H ETRUN.	

Army Form C. 2118.

WAR DIARY
or
INTELLIGENCE SUMMARY.
(Erase heading not required.)

45

Place	Date	Hour	Summary of Events and Information	Remarks and references to Appendices
ARRAS	25/4/18		Enemy shelled 3rd System Whilst on a working party No 122206 Pte McMORAN W. was killed by shell fire. Intermittent enemy barrage entirely S.O.S. was thrown up by CORPS on our right at 9:30 pm	222
"	26/4/18		1 & 2 Sections relieved 3 & 4 Sections in the Forward Outposts our both sides Casualties nil.	222
"	27/4/18		Battalion received Enemy shelled MONCHY & LES FOSSES FARM. Everything nil would continued on 3rd System	222
"	28/4/18		Situation normal Everything nil. Wallow road infront at night 2/Lt PSPAGE proceeded to U.K. on 14 days leave.	222

A 5834 Wt. W4973/M687 750,000 8/16 D. D. & L. Ltd. Forms/C.2118/13.

OPERATIONS - YPRES - 31.7.17. to 4.8.17.

MACHINE GUNS.

1. The Machine Guns attached to this Division for the operations numbered 80.

2 (i) Machine Gun Barrage of 32 guns was arranged for the operations commencing on the 31st July.
This was divided into 2 Groups, each group consisting of 2 Batteries of 8 guns.
Each Battery fired 6 barrages :- 3 from original positions - 1800 yards, 2400 yards and 2200 yards. They then moved forward and fired 2 more at 1800 yards and 2300 yards and then went on another 700 yards to put down a final barrage and S.O.S. line beyond the 3rd or final objective.

(ii) Owing to the enemy having direct observation and hostile aeroplane flying low over our lines almost daily, it was decided not to attempt to dig positions.
The 4 original battery positions were chosen and each gun position was marked with a wooden platform and on the last night all that had to be done was to place the tripod on it, aiming posts, due East for their ZERO mark having also been put out.

3. During the last three weeks before the operation, the following had been dumped at the positions :-

    480,000 Rounds S.A.A. in boxes.
    128,000   --do--   in 512 Belt boxes.
    30 Gallons oil.
    128 Petrol tins water.
    62 Elephant shelters for putting over the guns the last night.
    Aiming posts.
    Posts to mark positions of batteries.

In addition, material for 5 shelters had to be carried up and shelters made. Work was greatly hindered by hostile shell fire and gas shells, which on some nights stopped all working parties. Over 150 boxes S.A.A., 100 Belt Boxes, 4 Drums oil and several tripod platforms were destroyed by hostile shell fire, but an equal number of each were again taken up and all were in position by Y/Z night.

4. All guns carried out their programmes at the original position although coming under heavy hostile shell fire, 131,000 rounds were fired in the 3 barrages.
Guns were then cleaned and new barrels put in and the teams moved forward.
All teams got to their correct 2nd position except "B" Battery who were the last to move and owing to the heavy hostile barrage between WILDE WOOD and BELL COTTAGE got split up. 3 Guns eventually got into their correct positions and 3 guns to the South of the Railway. New Q E and direction were worked out and all fired according to programme.
Rounds fired 73,000.
The guns then proceeded to move forward to final position but owing to (a) heavy barrage put down by the enemy on the line between SQUARE FARM and FREZENBERG (b) the uncertain reports received as regards the actual position of our own troops on the Right, A and B Batteries took up positions about half way between 2nd and 3rd positions and came into action there. "C" were too far to the North and about 300 yards short and D got to their correct positions.

Where required.........

(2).

where required new calculations were made and all fired a certain number of rounds, but owing to the shortage of ammunition they did not all complete the programme.

5. AMMUNITION SUPPLY. This was the greatest difficulty especially "B" and "C" Batteries, who went into action in some cases with only 5 O.R. per team owing to :-

(a) Having no carriers attached
(b) Casualties suffered during the time they were in the line and on working parties. Every endeavour was made to get up S.A.A. Pack mules were used and got to the original position by 5.30 a.m. to help carry forward to 1st position, but owing to heavy hostile shell fire, the majority bolted or were wounded etc.

Each battery had a limber with 50 extra belt boxes, which got up to our own front line by 6 a.m. but could get no further. Boxes were dumped there.

The Infantry gave all assistance possible and ammunition was collected from wounded and odd boxes lying around. Each man as he moved forward also took 3 bandoliers slung round him.

The supply of ammunition was found difficult once the guns moved forward. Each team should consist of 1 N.C.O. and 8 O.R. to ensure sufficient ammunition being with the gun.

6. GUNS WITH ADVANCING BRIGADES. Each Brigade had 16 guns attached.

The Right Bde. had 8 with battalions who took up positions in strong points and the front line and 8 in reserve.

The left Brigade had the same and they were employed in the same way.

Those in the BLACK LINE (which became the front line, when the troops had to fall back a bit to conform with the Divisions on our right and left) did great execution in the repeated counter attacks, especially 2 guns about 200 yards in front of the FREZENBERG LINE at D.25.d.0.7. which gave great assistance during the heavy counter attack about 2 p.m. on the 1st inst.

The Brigade going through had all its 16 guns.

Each Battalion had 2 guns attached; 4 to do barrage from Black Line and 4 in Reserve.

Of the guns that went forward 4 got to Hill 37 and opened direct fire on the enemy. In a very short time only one gun was left in action. This remaining gun first covered a gap on our left, then covered the infantry when they retired, remaining in position till all ammunition was expended and the enemy within 20 yards of the gap.

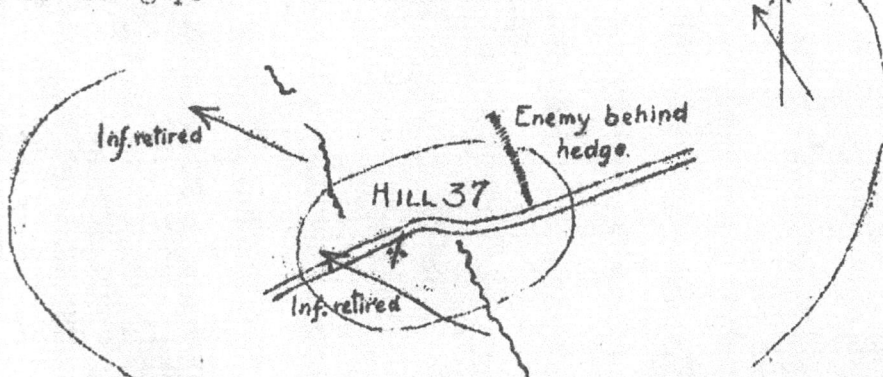

The number 1 was killed whilst endeavouring to carry the gun back. The only ones to get back being 1 Officer and 2 O.R. This officer again did excellent work with 2 more guns of another team in a position about 200 yards North of BECK HOUSE assisting to beat off all counter attacks from there until they were withdrawn on the 3rd inst.

Two more guns............

(3).

Two more guns were in BECK HOUSE and did great execution in the counter attacks, firing until they were surrounded, only 2 men getting back. The officer was last seen standing up firing his revolver with the Germans only 10 yards off.

Reports that the enemy were massing for counter attacks were frequent through the 1st and 2nd insts. and on each occasion all grouped guns fired on the area given. 10 guns were in SQUARE FARM, 6 behind GREY RUIN and 8 in IBEX RESERVE.

7. GENERAL. The mud and water made it extremely difficult to keep the guns clean, and nearly all had to be kept mounted all the time in the open without any cover, which accounts for the large number of guns damaged or completely destroyed by shell fire.

8. Harassing fire was carried out nightly during the Bombardment by 16 guns.

9. COMMUNICATIONS. Telephone was through to WILDE WOOD by 6.30 a.m. and to SQUARE FARM before 8 a.m. on the 31st inst. and was maintained until the end. Forward of that, runners were employed and all showed great determination in getting their message through.

10. REPAIR SHOP, was formed by an Armourer Staff Sergeant and all artificers in the School house and was very successful, over 12 guns being repaired there and sent forward again.